SELF-IMPROVEMENT THROUGH
PRACTICAL PSYCHOLOGY

An explanation of what psychology is and how it can be
applied in a practical way to the development of an
effective personality

SELF IMPROVEMENT THROUGH PRACTICAL PSYCHOLOGY

by
R.W. WILDE, M.A., B.Sc., Ph.D.

A. THOMAS AND COMPANY
Wellingborough, Northamptonshire

First published by The Psychologist Magazine Ltd.
as *Self-Improvement Through Practical Psychology* 1973
This Edition 1977
Second Impression 1980

ISBN 0 85454 044 X

Printed and bound in Great Britain
by Hunt Barnard Printing Ltd., Aylesbury, Bucks.

Contents

Foreword

AS the author of this book suggests, we are all to some degree psychologists, since anyone who has tried to understand what it is that motivates Man will in essence have involved himself with the science of psychology, or in other words will have studied the nature of the human mind.

Our approach will perhaps have been rather philosophical, somewhat like the ancient thinkers, as we have asked ourselves what it is that makes us what we are, and why it is that we feel as we do about certain things. We may well have resigned ourselves to the existing situation, saying: 'I am what I am, and nothing will change me.'

This is where we make the big mistake, and it is where modern psychology can both prove us wrong and at the same time promise us things which we would not have dreamed were within our grasp.

Psychological research, based upon systematic observation of the human mind, has proved that the mind possesses powers far beyond those generally called upon by the ordinary person. From this discovery springs the secret of success by which we can train ourselves to draw upon our full potential and go forward to a more fulfilling and happier life.

The secret lies in an understanding of oneself, and in an enthusiastic and active pursuit of high ideals. It lies also in a sweeping out of negative attitudes and an implanting in the mind of a positive vision of the better person we really want to be.

This book explains briefly the development of psychology from the ancient Greek philosophers to modern times, and goes on to show how the findings of the more scientific 'new psychology' can help us to build up our self-confidence and become better and more successful human beings.

Preface

ALL of us would like to be bigger and braver and happier people than we are and psychology can tell us something of the ways in which to go about achieving these aims.

Character is not formed in a day; nor is personality born overnight. We must be reasonably patient, and reasonably persistent, if we are to build up a *self* that is worth having.

Not even psychology can help a man over sheer laziness or indifference, but, given patience and the will to keep on trying, we can learn much from the discoveries of modern psychology.

It can put us on the right road. It can tell us how to go about this business of creating a worth-while self. It can save us from running up blind alleys.

Just how it can do this, I have tried to set down in this book.

It is a great and fascinating business, this building up of a self or personality. It is easily the most fascinating thing on earth and it is certainly the most rewarding.

Nobody can take from you your *self*. You can lose your money; you can (by separation or death) lose your friends; fame is a whimsical and uncertain thing; even health cannot always be secured. All these are, to a large extent, at the mercy of time and circumstance.

But *each of us can grow a self,* and there is no unlucky stroke of fate that can take *that* from us. That is the one unassailable possession; and we can go on adding to it to the last day of life.

Moreover, this pursuit of a worth-while self can keep life fascinating to the very end. Engaged in this, we need never be bored or dull or feel life empty.

Well over two thousand years ago Socrates spoke words that contain some of the greatest wisdom to which man can attain:

'*I do nothing but go about persuading you all, old and young alike, not to take thought for your persons, or your properties, but first and chiefly to care about the greatest improvement of the soul.*'

Three centuries later one even greater than Socrates put to his contemporaries the question: '*What shall it profit a man if he shall gain the whole world, and lose his own self?*'

Our aim should be the achievement of an ever finer 'selfhood' or personality. That is our duty to ourselves, no less than to others.

If anything in this book should help those who read it to adventure a little farther along the road to fine and victorious living, its author will be more than repaid.

R.W. Wilde

1.
Psychology — Old and New

PSYCHOLOGY is both very old and very new. In one sense it is almost as old as mankind, yet in another sense it is as new as space travel.

For psychology is the study of the mind. It is an attempt to get behind the physical man, and to understand things like thoughts and wishes, motives and desires, memories and feelings.

Ever since man started life on this planet he must have been, in some measure, a psychologist. For there can never have been a time when he did not try to understand himself and his fellows.

Why did someone act just like this, and not like that? Why is this man so different from that? Why do I find myself doing this thing, when all the time I really want to do that?

These, and a thousand similar questions, must have forced themselves upon human beings from the very beginning. And in so far as they came up against these questions, and tried to answer them, they were psychologists. Without ever having heard the word, they were (unknowingly) studying psychology.

Like other kinds of human questionings this thing, which began as a crude and vague inquiry in the early childhood of the race, slowly took on clearer shape and definition.

Even as far back as the time of Aristotle, who lived in Ancient Greece from 384 to 322 B.C., psychology was already a well-established subject of study. And ever since that time philosophers have pondered just what the *mind* might be, and how it works.

But modern psychology — sometimes called the 'New Psychology' — is not yet a century old. It appeared somewhere about the year 1890.

To understand the difference between the old and the new psychology, it is necessary to remember that at one time psychology was the province of the philosophers. That is to say, it was 'arm-chair' psychology.

Gifted thinkers would sit down in their study chairs and, by examining as keenly as they could the workings of their own minds, would write down what they discovered, and so try to formulate the 'laws' of the mind.

This keen detached study of one's own mind is called 'introspection.' And a number of valuable truths were discovered by this introspective process.

Modern psychology began by breaking away from this method of the study chair. It began to dawn upon certain thinkers that psychology could not hope to get very far by such a method.

If you want to study the workings of the human body, they said, you do not sit down in a study chair. You get into a laboratory or an operating theatre. If you want to study chemistry, you do not do it simply by reflective thinking. You start work with test tubes, Bunsen burners, balances and the like. Why not try these scientific, experimental, methods in psychology also?

Thus was modern psychology born. Two great names stand out in this break-away from philosophical arm-chair psychology. They are Wilhelm Max Wundt in Germany and William James in America.

In the later years of the 19th century Wundt opened in Germany the first psychological laboratory ever devised, and William James opened one a little later in America. Modern experimental psychology – the 'new psychology' – was beginning.

A third great name should be mentioned in speaking of the rise of the new psychology.* This is Sigmund Freud, of Vienna. Freud came to psychology from medicine.

He was, in 1890, a young nerve specialist, studying the origins and processes of the nervous system. He soon came to the conclusion that the nervous system could be influenced by the mind.

* Some writers reserve the name 'New Psychology' for psycho-analysis alone.

In the closing years of the last century he began to publish his books dealing with the unconscious mind, and *psycho-analysis*, another great feature of modern psychology, was born.

Since then, psychology has made rapid strides and it is studied in most of the major universities of the world.

This new psychology is affecting human life at many points. It has coloured our novels and our plays; it has influenced education; it has invaded the realm of medicine.

Articles upon it appear frequently in newspapers and magazines. Many thousands of books are written on it in many languages. It has thrown light upon many human problems. It has helped people to understand themselves and their fellows better.

In the succeeding chapters of this book we shall try to set down some of its more significant findings — those which appear most helpful to ordinary men and women in their search for guidance and power in daily living.

POINTS TO REMEMBER

1. — Psychology, in one sense, is as old as man, for it is man's attempt to understand the workings of mind — his own mind, and his fellow men's

2. — For many centuries psychology was simply 'introspective', and was a part of philosophy.

3. — The new psychology aims at studying

psychology along practical and experimental lines. It makes use of laboratories and apparatus. Introspection forms only a small part of its method.

4. – The founders of the new psychology were Wilhelm Wundt (in Germany) and William James (in America) who set up the first psychological laboratories; and Sigmund Freud (in Vienna) who invented psycho-analysis.

5. – The new psychology is being applied to education, medicine, and various other sciences. It has thrown much light on human motives and conduct.

2.
The Knowing Side of Life

MENTAL life has three phases or aspects. There is knowing; there is feeling; and there is willing (which produces action). In this chapter we shall deal with the *knowing* side of life.

By *knowing* psychologists do not mean just intellectual knowledge. They mean rather awareness. At every moment of our life, things are pressing upon us for our attention.

A man who is asleep or unconscious is scarcely aware at all; he is indifferent to the thousand and one things that are there to be seen and heard and noticed.

He who is dull and stodgy is aware of only a fraction of what life is at any moment presenting to him.

The average sort of person takes in more than the dull and stodgy one, but again is alive to only a small part of what is there to be noted and experienced.

The person who is intensely alive and alert takes in most. His life is the fullest; his world is the richest; his experience is the most intense and most fascinating.

It is worth noting that the world is the same for all of these people. It is the same world that is presenting itself to the sleeper, to the dull stodgy person, to the average person, and to the one who is keyed-up and alive.

It is not the world that is different. It is the people who are apprehending that world. Which leads to an important psychological truth:

Our world is what we make it. It depends upon the richness and vitality of our mind. We SEE *what we have the* POWER *of seeing.*

Most of us could be much more alive and alert than we are. Just test yourself out.

Think of one of your closest friends.
What is the colour of his eyes?
On which side does he part his hair?
In which pocket does he keep his handkerchief?
What is his usual colour in ties?

If you can answer these four questions off-hand, and correctly, you are among the more alive and receptive sort of people. But many who read this book will not be able to answer these four questions at all.

On the other hand, note the enthusiast. What an itense world is his, so far as his immediate hobby or purpose is concerned!

A schoolboy whose imagination has been caught by aircraft will tell you the type of a plane even at a distance. The man who collects butterflies has entered into a whole world of marvel and interest that is shut to most of us. Your film fan has collected a multitude of facts about the cinema.

A further significant fact is this — that these three, each an enthusiast in his field, have picked up this knowledge with but little conscious effort on their part. They have entered into a larger world without any great mental strain. Their interest has made learning easy.

TAKE AN INTEREST

So the golden rule for picking up knowledge, or mastering any particular subject, is: *inject interest into that subject.*

Key-up your awareness by interest, and knowledge becomes comparatively easy.

It is better if the interest so imported is a natural and immediate one. But in some cases, it has to be a distant and imagined one.

The schoolboy who has to master Greek irregular verbs for instance, will find it difficult to find an immediate interest in these perverse forms of speech! But if he can conjure up in his mind the glories of Ancient Greece, think how this was the speech of Socrates, of Plato, and of Alexander, a new enthusiasm may invade his task and transform drudgery into wonder.

Or he may perhaps look forward in anticipation to his future career, think of the mastery of Greek verbs as a further step towards his ambition to be a doctor, a scientist, a writer, and borrow from these ultimate ends a glory for the present task.

Whatever the means adopted, the principle is clear: Life grows in scope, in richness, in worth, as we go to it with something of the spirit of the enthusiast. By means of this, even humdrum tasks can be lightened, and real burdens made easy to carry.

BUILD-UP YOUR WORLD

Remember, that you are all the time building your world. The world you live in is that which you choose to apprehend.

Now there are various systems in vogue for heightening this faculty of awareness. Various exercises are suggested for improving the memory, or increasing awareness. Many of these are highly artificial. It is better to improve one's faculties in a natural way, and with the material that is ready to hand

Are you shy and sensitive and withdrawn? Begin to take a new interest in people. Take a new interest in them for their own sake. Note their ways, their habits, their mannerisms, their dress, their speech, their favourite topics, their ways of approaching this subject or that.

Do all this, not with the critical and fault-finding eye of the cynic, but with a desire genuinely to find people interesting, and to increase your world of personalities. It can be a very fascinating game, and in the process you will grow less shy, and more kind and tolerant.

There are very few people indeed who have not some likeable or admirable qualities.

IMPROVING THE MEMORY

Similarly with the memory. Do not worry yourself with artificial memory systems. Set your memory to work on the material ready to your hand in day-by-day experience.

You will at times be introduced to people. Try to remember their names. There are few things that give more innocent pleasure to people, than to find that someone, who met them only casually some time ago, now remembers them, on the next meeting, by name.

How is one to remember names? The answer is: by associating the name and the person, and investing both with 'interest'. Here is a man introduced to you by the name of Chambers. You notice that he has a rather 'legal' type of face. He looks rather like a barrister, or judge. Judge! There you have it. Judges sometimes adjudicate 'in chambers'. So your little mental note runs: Legal face, barrister, judge, *Chambers*.

Run over the list once or twice, and thereafter you will find it hard not to remember both name and face.

If this seems artificial to you, notice how, in some other case, your memory does actually work. It works by means of associations. It links up known with unknown. Which is precisely what you have done here. So long as the associations are easy and natural, and not forced, you are cultivating memory in a natural way. You are training a faculty along natural lines. And though the links may be trivial, the result is sound.

People not infrequently complain that they have 'lost their memory', or that they can no longer 'concentrate'. Short of some actual breakdown of the brain cells (which is exceedingly rare), the trouble nearly always goes back to one or two things. Either the person concerned has failed to cultivate memory; or he has come to doubt his power to remember or concentrate.

Even a muscle will go flabby if you do not use it; and many of us use our mental faculties far too little. But it is even more common to find people distrusting their minds. Our minds are like our friends: they live up, on the whole, to what we expect of them. Doubt them, and they draw away from us.

CONCENTRATION

People talk about concentration as if it were some weird, mystic, rare accomplishment, or something terribly hard and difficult to acquire. Many so-called 'mental systems' are founded on the same delusion.

Actually, concentration is the most natural thing in the world. The mind was made to concentrate, just as the stomach was made to digest, and the lungs to breathe.

You concentrate best, not by asking curious

questions about it, or by trying to examine yourself in the process, but simply by concentrating. If one part of your mind is looking at the rest of your mind concentrating, you have a divided mind; whereas concentration should be a whole-mind business, as natural, artless and simple as eating or breathing.

Do not distrust your mind. Take it for granted. Assume that nature has given you an instrument suited to its purpose. And, with that wholesome confidence, improve your power to remember or concentrate simply *by* remembering or concentrating.

Finally, let us note that 'the mind is the measure of the man'. We are as old as we feel. We are as happy as we think. We live in a world, impoverished or rich, which our mind has built up and singled out from all that is there. The more keenly we are alive, the more we take in, the more heightened our interest, the more polished our faculty of awareness – then the larger and fuller the world which we inhabit.

To the keenly aware mind the world need never be boring. There is a wealth of interest ready to hand. Determine to wake up, and LIVE!

Enlarge your frontier. Look up, and out, and learn. Glean knowledge from whatever you can. Every new piece of knowledge acquired enlarges your mind, and so enlarges YOU!

Do not pass through this miracle of life with eyes bandaged, ears clogged and mind asleep. Use your mind – it was meant to be used. Trust

it — and you will find it trustworthy. Be alert —
the universe is at your door.

And the reward? Just that you grow — grow
in wisdom, in knowledge, in richness of experience. Just that you live in a happier, wider
world.

It is the mind that maketh good or ill,
That maketh wretch or happy, rich or poor.

POINTS TO REMEMBER

1. — *Each of us makes a world that is pecu-*
liarly his, or her, own. Our 'world' is that which
our mind takes in.

2. — *Interest is the golden key to learning,*
remembering, and the like. Where we cannot
find an immediate interest, we can inject one by
imagination and forward-looking vision.

3. — *Concentration is a natural faculty. It*
grows by exercise. The mind works best when
trusted.

4. — *We are as big as our mind. Every growth*
in knowledge, awareness, interest, means a
growth in personality.

3.

Your Feelings

THE second phase or aspect of mental life is, we said, *feeling*. We do only think; we *feel*. We are creatures not only of intellect, but also of emotion.

What has modern psychology to say about this realm of feeling?

Firstly this: that *feeling is the great driving-power of life*. Feeling is to human personality what petrol is to the motor-car, steam to the railway-engine. No man ever lived wisely without the use of intelligence. But no man ever lived strongly without the aid of emotion.

There are circles in which it is customary to decry emotion. It is a sign of weakness, or of bad form, it is said. In some quarters social discipline aims at avoiding all display of feeling, and at maintaining an even veneer of placidity. The ideal, it is suggested, is to meet every experience with the same urbane demeanour.

Now there is a partial truth underlying all such notions. It is that emotional riot is both unlovely and profitless. The woman who, in some emergency or crisis, merely lies on the floor and screams and kicks, is allowing certain emotions free play. But she is not merely a rather disgusting spectacle; she is decidedly in the way — in the way of those who are trying to meet the emergency or crisis with practical common sense and intelligence.

Emotion out of hand is a dangerous force. It unfits us for wise and appropriate action. That is why it is silly to lose your temper; you not only display your own lack of self-control, but you also prevent yourself from meeting the annoying situation in a practical manner. When you lose your temper, you lose *yourself* — the self that is worth having.

In the same way ungoverned fear precludes profitable action. In extreme cases, it even acts so as to paralyse arms or legs, and keeps us rooted in the spot just where danger threatens.

It is this recognition that emotion out of hand is dangerous that has led some thinkers to hold up the ideal of never displaying emotion at all. It is this which lies behind the cult of urbanity. This it is which explains why, in certain circles, any show of emotion at all is bad form.

Bur all this is only taking one dose of poison as cure for some different poison! Be assured of this: no man ever lived strongly, or worked mightily for the world's benefit, who was not moved by deep and strong emotion. To shut off emotion is to shut off the great driving-force for finest and most worth-while living.

Think, for instance, what we said in the previous chapter about interest. Interest is a feeling-experience, and where interest is present tasks otherwise forbidding become bearable and even likeable. Think, again, how love can transform a human personality, so that the lover literally walks in a new world, a world wondrously more fragrant and beautiful.

Think how patriotism has called men to unimaginable heights of heroism and endurance. And think how religious emotion has led men and women, on the one hand, to unflinching and uncalculating martyrdom, and, on the other hand, to acts of boundless compassion and mercy towards the unfortunate and the weak, and even towards the wicked and repellent.

Under the impulse of fine emotion we can rise to heights which we never could scale by the aid of cold reasoning alone. The power to feel deeply is essential to all worth-while living.

So that what we must aim at is something midway between the two extremes — midway between a total *inhibiting* of all emotion and the free and riotous *display* of emotion. We must discipline our emotion, but not stultify it. In a word, our aim should be to guide emotion by intelligence.

We should think intelligently, and act emotionally. By which we mean that we should decide by clear reason and intelligent reflections just what things are worth doing in life, just what goals are worth pursuing, and then, to the doing and the seeking of these things, we should bring all our richest powers of emotion and feeling.

To think clearly, and to feel deeply — these are two elements in all victorious living.

ENCOURAGE BETTER EMOTIONS

This leads us to a further point. It is apparent to all of us that some emotions are more worth living with than others. It is better to live with love than with hate, with courage than with fear, with hope than with despondency, with patience than with bad temper, with tolerance than with narrow-mindedness.

How we feel profoundly affects us. The emotions that most commonly claim us decide in large measure what sort of persons we are.

But how are we to encourage the better emotions, and eliminate the poorer ones? Can we control at all how we feel? Or do feelings 'just come', regardless of what we may think or wish?

One principle we must make clear at the outset. You cannot kill any emotion merely by thinking about it, nor even by gritting your teeth and trying to force it out of your mind. Anyone who has tried to do that with some strong emotion has found how unsuccessful such a course can be.

No, you cannot kill an emotion by attacking it directly: but you can expel it by a flank attack. You can rout it by bringing in its opposite emotion.

You can make use of what William James called 'the expulsive power of a new affection.' To get rid of an undesirable emotion you must cultivate its opposite. If you are prone to hate, you must cultivate love; if you are constantly fearful, you must cultivate courage.

But how is one to cultivate a desirable emotion? There are two ways.

The first is by dwelling upon the desired emotion in thought, seeing it as desirable, picturing oneself in imagination as possessing it.

Here books are a great help. To read of heroic deeds is already to find one's stores of courage growing. Similarly to make contact with persons who themselves possess the kind of emotions we wish to acquire, is to catch the fire.

Imagination, as we shall see at a later point in this book, is a potent force. To wish greatly for some quality, is already to be on the way towards possessing it. To picture oneself as having it, to imagine what one would be like when having it, is to set forces working in the mind that bring that quality more within our reach.

The second method is a practical one. *It is to act as if we really did possess the desired quality, as if the wished-for emotion were really present with us.*

Try a little experiment with yourself. Next time you are feeling particularly glum and gloomy, take the first opportunity to speak some cheery word to someone — milkman, postman, workfellow, or acquaintance. Say the cherry word as if you meant it thoroughly; throw your shoulders back; lift up your face into a smile; and — *speak the cheery word.*

You will be surprised to find, looking back, that a new cheerfulness in that very moment began to break through your own spirit! In short, we can induce emotions, to a large extent, by bodily action.

Act, in a bodily way, the emotion you desire, and you open a gateway through which that emotion can come. Act out the feeling, and you will find the feeling beginning to creep in.

All this is not some nice arm-chair theory. It has been tested out in psychological laboratories. It has been confirmed again and again in the experience of ordinary men and women. Thousands of people have changed themselves from timid, distrustful, fearful, individuals into confident and courageous personalities.

One final word on this matter of feeling. It is not only the thoughts we think, but also the feelings that we most often indulge in, that make us what we are. It pays to live with the best emotions. And *we can choose our emotions.*

We can cultivate a certain type of emotion, just as we can cultivate a certain type of friend. We should choose both with intelligence and care.

POINTS TO REMEMBER

1. — It is a mistake to suppress all emotion.

Emotion is the great driving-power of living.

2. — But emotion should not be an undisciplined riot. Feelings should be strong and deep, but they should be guided and directed by intelligence.

3. — Our aim should be to think clearly; to decide by reason what things we intend to pursue in life; and then to act with rich and sustained emotion.

4. — We need not be slaves to any particular emotion. We can cultivate a certain type of emotion, just as we can cultivate a certain type of friend.

5. — Live with the best emotions. Our feelings make us what we are.

4.

The Psychology of Will

WE come in this chapter to the third phase or aspect of mental life — the aspect of *willing*. That process by which the mind chooses which of two or more alternatives it will pursue, and then follows up that choice by action.

What help can psychology give on this subject of will?

One thing we should be aware of is that it is natural for the mind to be able to will. That sounds trite and obvious. Yet it is frequently ignored or doubted.

People talk, and act, as if willing was a rare accomplishment, utterly foreign to ordinary human nature as such. But willing is just as natural as thinking or feeling. The mind was made to will.

I write this because in many books all sorts of fantastic exercises are devised for the 'strengthening of the will'.

For example, one is bidden to count up to several hundreds at the rate of one number per second, checking the timing with a watch, and starting all over again if one begins to count too quickly. Or one is told to tangle up a ball of wool in the most intricate way possible, and then slowly disentangle it. Or again, one is instructed to put some peas in a bottle and patiently take them out one by one and count them.

Such exercises may encourage patience, but they can scarcely do much to strengthen will!

With will, as with concentration, it is better to train oneself in the actual circumstances of ordinary living, and not conjure up fantastic and artificial situations or exercises.

The fact is that we are *willing* every day of our lives. At a thousand turns in any ordinary day we decide this as against that, do this thing instead of the other. It is all so common and so usual that we never think of this as willing at all.

It is only when we are faced with some big and momentous choice that we think of our will.

But common daily living gives us plenty of opportunity to exercise our will, if we care.

Another fact is this — that will is most characteristically human. Animals think, to some extent; they certainly feel. But they seem to have little or no power of will. They act on impulse. Even the child has small powers of will; he too is very much moved by impulse. But with manhood or womanhood we become capable of full-grown will. We can, if we care, control mere impulse, and choose our course of action by an effort of will.

EXERCISE YOUR WILL-POWER

How can we improve our power of will? The answer is: we can improve will just as we improve any other faculty — by exercising it.

The more you exercise it, the greater grows your power of will. Every good piece of willing makes another good piece of willing easier.

This is not to say that we are to conjure up terrific powers of will in face of every trivial and simple matter. We should suit the amount of will to the situation. The man who sits in a teashop, debating for five minutes with himself whether he will have a bath bun or a doughnut, is not exercising his will profitably; he is wasting time.

We should not hear the machinery of our mind creaking too loudly. To make will terribly self-conscious in this way is not to improve it, but to fuddle it.

Moreover, if the advice I have given in the two previous chapters is followed, the will's functioning will already have become easier. If we have built up the habit of looking out clearly upon life, and deciding by quiet reason just what aims are most worth pursuing; and if we have then brought to these our stores of feeling and emotion, the process of willing will already have become very largely an automatic and subconscious thing.

Think of what we mean by character. We mean by it a certain persistence and a certain consistency. The man of character is not fickle and variable; he is steady and reliable. You could almost predict what he will do in a given situation.

So a man who is thoroughly honest will not toy with the thought of stealing; his will functions almost automatically here; there will be no great effort about it. So the pure woman could not act impurely; purity is so much a part of her character that her will runs easily and smoothly in the direction of purity.

All this is just as it should be. There is no virtue in creaking machinery. The efficient machine runs smoothly. Our wills are at their best *when they decide easily and consistently the things which in our best moments we should wish them to decide.*

OUR IDEAL SELF

This brings us to a further point. Away behind all acts of will there lies our conception of our ideal self — the self we should wish to be. Faced by two alternatives, our will should decide for that which is most in harmony with our ideal self. And the clearer our conception of what we wish to be; the more vivid our picture of our ideal self, the more easy will the act of willing become.

Go out to life having in your mind a picture of the man or woman you wish to be. And, when the need for some real choice confronts you, take that course which is most in line with that picture of your wished-for self.

These broad directions having been laid down,

is it possible to suggest detailed ways of strengthening will?

We have already spoken against highly artificial and fantastic exercises to this end. There are, however, two principles which we should do well to recognize, and practise, if we desire to strengthen our power of will.

The first of these is that we should go out of our way, as it were, to exercise our will occasionally. That is, we should bring ourselves to forgo inclination or impulse, where it would not be wrong to follow it, for the sheer sake of bringing our will into play.

If you are a cigarette smoker, for example, you might occasionally decide to go for a whole day without a cigarette. If you are very prone to chocolates, you might forgo these for a while.

There is nothing morally wrong in smoking or in eating chocolates; in the ordinary way we can give rein to such impulses with a good conscience. But occasionally to do a thing, for the sole reason that we would rather not do it, is a very real means of strengthening our power of will.

FOLLOW WILL WITH ACTION

The second principle is that we should lose no time in following up any decision of will by action. We should not let the grass grow between choice and action. We should give no time for mere impulse, or self-indulgence, or simple laziness, to get between will and deed. There are very solid reasons for such a counsel.

It is one thing to have an idea in the mind; it is another to link that idea up with those areas in the brain that control our muscles and limbs. The second is an altogether stronger and more far-reaching process than the first. It makes a deeper tract within the brain. To follow up will consistently by action is to create many such tracts, and to build the elements of stable character.

There is one further point which must be considered in connection with this matter of willing. Once having made your decision, after a careful survey of all the facts, and having come to that choice which seems to you (in all the circumstances) wisest and best, *stick to your choice, and waste no regrets if afterwards you find you were mistaken.*

Of course if it is still possible to alter things, alter them by all means if you have been proved wrong.

But where the matter has gone beyond recall, do not disturb your peace of mind by tormenting yourself with the reflection that, if you had known *then* all that you know *now*, you would have chosen differently. There are people who have broken themselves by such a mistaken practice. It is utterly futile and unreasoning.

None of us is infallible. We can only choose as wisely and as honestly as we can, with the facts which are at our disposal at the moment when we choose. Even should things afterwards turn out badly, we have nothing to reproach ourselves with. We have done the best we could; and even archangels cannot do more than that.

Have, then, the courage of your convictions. Dare to make your choice. Having made it, act upon it. And afterwards waste no time on regrets.

Will, like thought and feeling, is meant to be used. Like them, it is meant also to be used with courage and confidence.

POINTS TO REMEMBER

1. — *The act of willing is a natural process of mind. It is not some strange or unnatural art.*

2. — *Character is built up by willing consistently in the same directions.*

3. — *Will is strengthened, like all other faculties, by being exercised.*

4. — *The clearer the picture in our mind of the self we wish to be, the easier will it be for us to will in the right direction.*

5. — *It is good occasionally to control impulse by will, for the sheer sake of strengthening will.*

6. — *We should lose no time in following up decision by action.*

7. — *Having decided, as wisely as we could, we should not reproach ourselves later with regrets if fresh facts come to light.*

5.
The Unconscious Mind

CONSCIOUS processes of mind are by no means the whole story. Much goes on in our minds below the level of consciousness. Each of us, in fact, possesses an unconscious mind, or, as it is often called, a sub-conscious mind.

The existence of the unconscious mind was largely the discovery of Sigmund Freud, and it has come to play an increasing part in psychological theory.

What exactly is the unconscious mind? And what is its function? We must not think of it as a second, or separate, mind. Briefly, we may say that the unconscious mind contains all those mental facts and feelings and ideas that are not present in the conscious mind. It is the great storehouse of memory.

Many memories we can, of course, bring into the conscious mind without difficulty. I can, by a little simple reflection, remember what I had for dinner yesterday. But other memories are gone beyond recall.

I cannot, by any effort of will, remember the things I said and did, or that were said and done to me, when I was two years old. Yet nothing once experienced is completely lost from the mind. Its effects linger on. They exist in that realm of unconscious memory which can no longer be opened up at will.

Now Freud has shown how significant it is that these memories of early childhood are sunk below the level of consciousness. It is significant for this reason: that we all begin life craving only ease, comfort, and pleasure. Or, in Freud's term, our infant mind is dominated by the 'pleasure principle.'

The young child desires only pleasure and safety. And he sees the things of his world, not as they really are, but as he wishes them to be. Only slowly, as the child develops, does another principle come into play — the 'reality principle.'

As this new principle gains ground, the individual is governed less by the desire for mere ease and comfort, and becomes willing to suffer pain and discomfort, if need be, for others' sakes, or in the service of his ideals. He no longer looks at the world through the distorting spectacles of wishes, but is able to see things as they really are.

So that human development, on the mental side, is very much a matter of the victory of the reality principle over the pleasure principle.

Only — and this is central to Freud's whole psychology — the pleasure principle is never entirely *killed*, so to speak. It lingers on and rears its head sometimes; so that, even as grown men and women, we never completely outgrow the craving for simple ease and pleasure and safety.

In weak personalities, the pleasure principle is more active. In mature personalities, it is the reality principle that dominates. Yet in both alike there is always a certain 'pull' from below, from the pleasure principle which was the governing factor in our childhood mentality. There is always a certain amount of effort in living up to the reality principle.

It is just this which explains why it is sometimes very hard to *will* the right thing. We know the better thing, yet we sometimes choose the worse. Even with the picture of our ideal self before us, we give way to simple laziness, or passion, or timidity. Perhaps we say of ourselves that we have a 'weak will.'

It should help all of us to realize that in all such cases it is simply our unabandoned childishness that is getting in the way. We simply have not grown up enough. And, because we have not completely grown up, we have not thrown off the influence of the old infantile yearning for ease and pleasure and safety.

In short, while we are born with an unconscious mind, dominated by the pleasure principle, a truly adult mind, controlled by intelligent purposes and worthwhile ideals, is something we have to achieve.

SELF UNDERSTANDING

In this realm, self-understanding is of great value. Many a man who agonizes over some bad habit or defect of character, and who talks mournfully about his 'weak will' or vicious tendencies, would come nearer the truth if he were to recognize that he is simply being a baby! He has not mentally grown up! It is his infantile mind which is master!

In certain really serious cases, where physical disorder is present, or where the mind is a prey to some really devastating habit, a process of 'analysis' may be called for. This is a method of treatment where a psychologist helps a patient to work backwards to discover just what hidden memories, just what old infantile 'pulls', are spoiling the patient's present health and happiness, and making it impossible for him to live like a truly grown-up and mature person.

The patient is led to see just where the old baby-ish mentality is spoiling his life, and, in the light of his new self-knowledge, he is able to face things with a grown-up mentality, governed by the reality principle.

But ordinary people do not need to be 'analysed.' In the case of most of us it is sufficient to know that the habits which spoil our peace of mind, the traits of character that are out of tune with our ideal self, are the outcome of old childish wishes, still not mastered by the willingness to face reality and to meet it on the adult level. Often enough a

little quiet reflection will enable us to trace
these old primitive impulses to their lair.

In some people these infantile traits are
obvious on the surface. Clearly enough the man
or woman who sulks and pouts; who resorts to
tears, or to violent tantrums at the slightest
provocation; who always demands his or her
own way; who is constantly eaten up with envy
and jealously; who sacrifices clear duty to mere
laziness or selfish indulgence; or is for ever
running away from every hard or unpleasant
fact, is simply meeting life at the level of
babyhood.

There are plenty of these grown-up children
in the world. At their mildest, they are pathetic;
at their worst, they are a positive social danger.

No one of us can live worthily and fruitfully
until he is prepared to be a grown-up person,
willing to look at facts rather than at wishes.
Real childhood has its own lovely and natural
qualities. But there is nothing likeable or admirable in a *grown-up* baby.

Such people are petty tyrants and social
destroyers. Their one ever-recurring question to
life is: 'What can I get out of it?' Selfishness is
their ruling motive. Their pathway is strewn
with the wrecks of marital unhappiness, broken
friendships, and spoiled relationships. They
make fruitful human co-operation impossible
Into every circle where they come, into every
association they enter, they bring strife, dis-
harmony, and disruption.

One condition of all worth-while personality

is that we shall be willing to grow up. This world is no place for sulking, puling babies. The really mature man and woman meet life at the grown-up level; recognize the rights and happiness of others as not less sacred than their own; and ask of life less 'what can I get out of it?' than 'what can I put into it?'

Unconscious, pleasure-governed, mentality is a gift: we are born with it. Mature, reality-governed mentality is an achievement; it is something we have to build. Our success and happiness hinge upon it.

POINTS TO REMEMBER

1. — The unconscious mind is the great store-house of memory.

2. — Many of these 'memories' are of childish happenings, ideas, and wishes.

3. — The ruling force in childhood is the pleasure principle.

4. — Hence, the unconscious mind is cruder and more childish than the conscious mind.

5. — Mature manhood and womanhood depend upon replacing the pleasure principle by the reality principle.

6. — We cannot have developed personalities unless we are willing to grow up.

6.
The Larger Self

IT might be thought, from what I have written in the previous chapter, that the unconscious mind is wholly mischievous, a source of weakness only.

This is far from being the case. Indeed, I hope to show in this chapter that it can be made a means of power. There are ways of utilizing the unconscious to improve our lives.

But before we go on to speak of this in detail, let us pause for a moment to note another profound and highly important fact:

We are all of us much bigger than we know. All the accumulated testimony of psychological investigation points to this. None of us comes near to using anything like the whole of the talents and powers and capacities we really possess. We have sources of strength and of power that we but rarely tap.

All this is true even on the purely physical level. Experiments go to show that, where a person's mind is keyed up to faith and confidence, even his physical capacities are decidedly enlarged.

The runner's 'second wind' is well-known. Under the stimulus of confidence we can exert a greater muscular effort. In the ordinary way, of course, we do not need to display phenomenal physical proficiency. We were not meant to work all the time at the outside limit. But — and this is the point — these unsuspected and 'extra' powers are there, and a certain mental attitude can call them into play.

Ordinarily, we do not even know they are there; very few of us ever make use of them.

It is the same story again where the sense organs are concerned. Our eyes can see much more than most of us ever allow them to see; our ears can hear sounds that ordinarily we never do hear. The sensitiveness of the blind man's fingers is proverbial. He has, under the stress of need, simply developed faculties that are there in all of us.

Countless experiments in psychological laboratories have revealed that we have powers of sight, hearing, touch, and the like, that seem utterly incredible. Only — we never make use of them.

What is true on the physical plane is no less true on the mental plane. Most of us are only a part of ourselves. The rest of us sleeps and is never called into being. We have powers and capacities and gifts that we scarcely dream of possessing. What might we become if these hidden resources were released, and we began to realize our full potential?

I am not suggesting or recommending mere boasting or swaggering, nor even a superficial over-confidence. Indeed, all such traits are a form of unreality: they are manifestations of that baby-mentality which we spoke about in the previous chapter.

The man who is quietly sure of himself does not boast; he gets on with the job. It is the man who, subconsciously at all events, is *not* sure of himself who boasts. He boasts to keep his courage up.

Psychology is no substitute for clear reason and common sense. A swaggering demeanour disguising an empty brain is like a toy balloon over-expanded. The merest touch will burst it.

But most of us are too distrustful of ourselves. We are afraid to launch out and develop our powers. We fail to make use of one-half of what we really are and possess. And it is to all such folk that modern psychology utters its encouragement. It tells them that they are much bigger people than they have ever dreamed; that they have gifts and capacities which they have scarcely touched the fringe of; that they have a potential self-hood larger by far than they have dared to believe.

THE MAGIC KEY

Where shall we find the magic key that will open the doorway through which we may pass to our finer self? I have thrown out hints of it here and there throughout this book. Now it may be summed up in three words: *enthusiasm, confidence, vision.*

By *enthusiasm* I mean a quality of emotion that will bring fire to our latent energies and stir them up to their best. Love is the greatest of all such emotions — love in its various forms.

All of us know what a mother will do for love; how, under stress of her child's sickness or danger, she will display unimaginable powers of daring or endurance. All of us know what the patriot will do for love of country. All of us know something of what has been done by the great lovers of mankind, the great pioneers and prophets and leaders of the race.

Men and women will do, and be able to do, for love, what otherwise they would never be able to achieve.

By *confidence* I mean a real trust in our powers to do what we feel called upon to do. I mean the throwing aside of our timidity and fearfulness and self-distrust, and a courageous willingness to go out to life, believing in ourselves, and launching forth hopefully upon this quest for self-discovery and self-development. I mean the quiet determination to make the best of ourselves — not simply for selfish reasons, but for others' sakes as well as our own.

And by *vision* I mean the frequent holding before ourselves of a picture of the man or woman we wish to be, the frequent conjuring up in our imagination of our ideal self. I mean some

4

real conception of the goals we mean to reach, the ambitions that shall guide our life, the things we desire to pursue and serve.

These three — enthusiasm, confidence, vision — are, of course, intimately bound up together. We can breed them by following the recommendations which this book has laid down. In particular, what is written in chapters 2 and 3 concerning interest and emotion is of importance here. In the next and final chapter, I shall have other hints to give.

AUTO-SUGGESTION

Before this, however, there is a word to say about utilizing the energies of the unconscious mind in the service of our best life. The way to do this is known technically as 'auto-suggestion.'

'Suggestion' rests upon the discovered fact that *any idea which really makes its way into the unconscious tends to be acted out.*

Just as old childish wishes and ideas, living on in the unconscious mind, still exert a 'pull' upon us, so new ideas and wishes planted there will also live on, and exert a new 'pull' in their turn. They, too, will enlist the energies of the unconscious towards their fulfilment.

Only, if such things are to take effect, they must really 'get through' to the unconscious mind. Let us put the matter in concrete terms. And let us put it in terms of a very simple and comparatively trifling circumstance.

Here is a young girl who bites her nails. How

is she to get rid of the habit? First, there must be the conscious approach. She must tell herself that this is a rather dirty and nasty habit, not only damaging to her appearance but also unpleasant to others. She must tell herself that she owes a duty to others, as well as to herself, to look her best.

She must see vividly how ugly and repellent are her fingers in their present condition. She must conjure up a picture of what her hands would look like, neatly manicured and daintily kept. And she must determine that she really will outgrow this ugly habit and subdue it. She must tell herself hopefully and confidently that it is within her power to make this change and realize her wish.

All this is the conscious approach. Here you have the three elements which we have spoken of earlier in this chapter — enthusiasm, confidence, and vision.

Yet, notwithstanding, the cure may 'hang fire'. With her best intentions, and in spite of her real desire, she may fail to conquer her nail-biting habit. Which, psychologically considered, means that the unconscious pull of the old pleasure principle is too much for her later, and in this case weaker, reality principle.

It is here that she can make use of a technique which attacks this pleasure principle *where it lives*, that is, in the unconscious mind. She can set the unconscious mind to work to modify itself. And she can do this by what is called auto-suggestion.

Each night when she is curled up in bed, when her body is restful and her mind drowsy, and she feels sleep is very near, then, without any attempt to rouse herself, let her whisper (in the softest possible fashion) inside herself, about sixteen to twenty times, these sentences:

'I am going longer and longer without biting my nails. This habit is getting weaker and weaker. My nails are becoming nicer. Soon I shall have nicely-shaped and well-kept hands.'

She must do this very drowsily, with no effort at concentration or hard thought, not more than some nineteen or twenty times at most and then let herself fall asleep. If she falls asleep while she is saying the suggestions, so much the better.

This must be done every night, over several months, but always in a sleepy, effortless, drowsy fashion, just mumbling the words over inside herself.

She need not reflect upon the process at all in wakeful hours. She can just leave the unconscious processes to go on by themselves in their own hidden fashion. She has set working forces in her mind that are subtler and deeper even than intellectual reflection and even ordinary will-power. The unconscious mind is very powerful.

Such is auto-suggestion. And it can deal with things far more serious and obstinate than nail-biting. By means of it countless men and women have thrown off the shackling habits of years, and have risen into a new and larger selfhood.

It should be remembered that auto-suggestion is not substitute for the enthusiasm, confidence, and vision we have spoken of — which are things of the conscious mind. It should be used along with these, to reinforce them and to do for the unconscious mind what these are doing for the conscious.

Against the combination of the two even the most stubborn habits and failings go down. When conscious and unconscious work together in the same direction you have a force that is irresistible.

POINTS TO REMEMBER

1. — We are each of us bigger than we know. *We have a larger self than we have ever yet discovered.*

2. — Enthusiasm, confidence, and vision, are the keys to this discovery of the larger self.

3. — Auto-suggestion taps the energies of the unconscious, and sets forces working there that have incalculable power.

7.
Psychology and Religion

MORE than once in this book we have touched upon goals, ambitions, aims, ideals, and the like. We have read something of what modern psychology has to say concerning the pursuit of these, and their realization. But we have never actually discussed precisely *what* goals and ambitions are most worth striving after, nor what ideals are most worth the holding.

When we come to such questions we step (strictly) beyond psychology into the realm of philosophy. Yet we cannot very well avoid going on to ask these further questions.

Even at the psychological level it is clear that some ideals are better than others, some character traits more worth possessing than others. It is better, for instance, to live by love than by hate: love expands the personality, while hate dwarfs and diminishes it. It is better to live by confidence than by fear; fear paralyses our efforts, while confidence enables us to reach out towards our finest powers. It is better to live by co-operation than by self-imposed isolation: man is a social animal, and never realizes his fullest life without enjoying harmonious relations with his fellows.

All this is clear from a psychological point of view. You might say that some emotions, some ambitions, some ideals *pay* while others do not.

But some cases are not so clear. What of self-sacrifice, self-denial, faithfulness even unto death? Do these pay? Are these to the advantage of the individual who practises them? Even here, in a sense it is possible to answer *yes*. You might say that these things, so fully exemplified in the greatest characters of history, were some of the ingredients of their splendid personalities.

Take away heroism, sacrifice and unselfish service from the pages of history and you lose the greatest sons and daughters of the race. Yet it seems a stretching of language and common sense to say that it *pays* some individual to go to martyrdom. If such conduct leads to happiness, it is a happiness which is different from what is commonly meant by the word.

Let us approach the problem from a rather different angle. We have spoken of enthusiasm, confidence and vision as the golden keys to enlarged selfhood. But there are circumstances in which such words must sometimes seem little more than empty sounds.

What of the man who has been out of work for years on end and who has no early prospect of finding work? Even with him, it is true that his world is what his mind takes in. But there will be some things in the world of his experience that he cannot well shut out.

What, again, of the parent whose only child is suddenly snatched away by death or accident? What of the individual whose husband or wife is dying slowly of some painful disease? And what of the victim of that disease?

Such cases are not isolated, even if they are (happily) comparatively rare. Pain and disaster are sufficiently woven into the scheme of things for none of us to evade sometimes asking questions about them. And he would be a bold psychologist who should go to the sort of people we have mentioned above, and tell them that enthusiasm, confidence, vision, would see them through and make all well.

There is yet a third way of stating our problem. In chapter 5 we discussed the reality principle as a factor in mental development. The truly grown-up man or woman, we learned, was at least one who was willing to face reality, and to react to life in terms of reality. But what *is* reality? What can psychology say about that?

The answer is that psychology as such can say nothing about it. It is philosophy which must answer that question. What reality means for you will be decided by your philosophy of life, or (to use another term) your religion.

RELIGIOUS ATTITUDE

Now it is precisely facts like these which led Dr. Carl Jung, the great Swiss psychoanalyst, to say that, looking back over many years of practice, he realized that he had never been able to cure any patient of serious psychological disorder, unless, he had been able to induce in that patient 'a religious attitude to life.'

Even here we are not entirely free of ambiguities. Not all of religion itself is based upon the reality principle. There are many people for whom religion is only an 'escape mechanism' — that is, a means whereby they run away from the hard and difficult and unpleasant facts of life.

They go to their God to be molly-coddled and kept safe. These are the people who, when trouble or disaster comes, ask whiningly: 'What have I done, that God should let this happen to *me*?' Such a religion is both psychologically bad, and, as a working philosophy, unsound.

Nor, again, do we mean by 'religion' a matter of creeds, dogmas and articles of faith. A man may recite every syllable of a creed, and yet live his life in a way that is completely irreligious. Religion is bigger than any creed, or all of them together.

When we turn to the great masters of the spiritual life we find that they are agreed upon certain fundamental things.

1. They are persuaded that this life is no puppet-play, but that its struggles are real struggles, and that real issues are being fought out according to the way we live, each of us, day by day.

2. They are persuaded that we are here in this world to grow a soul or self, and that everything we can experience, of good or of ill, may be made to contribute to that supreme purpose.

3. They are persuaded that truth, and goodness, and love, are not only desirable things, here and now (which psychology can testify), but that they have their place in an eternal order of things, and will one day be triumphant.

4. They are persuaded that each of us is here not simply to seek his (or her) own, but also to love and serve his fellows, and help build the kingdom of God upon earth.

5. They are persuaded that almighty love rules at the heart of things, and that everything (could we but see and know all) has its place and its function within a purpose of almighty love.

Now if all *this* be reality, then we know where we stand. It is not simply that love and kindness and courage *work* psychologically. We do not want to feel that we are not building our lives upon illusions, even though they are pleasant ones and pay decent dividends here and now in happiness and well-being.

Honest people do not like dope, even though it is pleasant. They want to feel that the psychology which works is itself linked up with the real truth of things and corresponds with reality about life and the universe.

PHILOSOPHY OF LIFE

So we come to this conclusion — that behind all

that modern psychology has to teach us concerning the way to health, happiness, and fullness of living, there is need for a philosophy of life, a religion, that squares with our psychology, and which itself leads us into reality. Seek the real, says psychology. But it is our philosophy of life, our religion, which decides what is the ultimate reality.

Now, nobody who knows anything about history would deny that men may live bravely and fruitfully even though their philosophy is one of stark pessimism, and their religious beliefs entirely negative. But deep down such courage and practical helpfulness must rest upon a kind of despair.

For the kindness, and honour, and fortitude such people display must, in their view, be alien things in a universe that does not care two hoots about them. To them, the things which human minds and hearts hold most precious have no significance at all in the universe at large, and will all end in smoke, so to speak.

But, on a religious view of life, the things which, in our best moments, we sense as highest and noblest, have their place in the eternal scheme of things, are wrought into the very structure of the universe.

Truth, beauty, goodness and love are not just qualities which we may strive to attain, and which die with us, but are the final and eternal truths about this universe in which we find ourselves. And the soul or personality we are struggling here to build is destined to go on increasingly growing and developing into powers and splendours that pass our present comprehension.

If we are really to follow our thought through, pursue our inquiry to its logical conclusion, we are bound to think our way through psychology on to philosophy and religion. We are bound to ask ourselves just what reality is. And there is no escaping the fact that it does make a tremendous difference the way we answer that question.

If the struggle is to be worth-while, and if the worst life can do to us is still to have a meaning, it will be because we take a 'religious' view of life — by which we mean that we accept the final broad fundamental persuasions that were outlined a few paragraphs back.

It is facts like these, forced home upon his mind after a lifetime of psychological practice and research, that led Dr. Jung to say that, in the last resort, it is a 'religious view of life' which is needed to establish complete mental harmony and well-being.

PURPOSE OF LIFE

So that the last word of this book must be that you are here for the growing of a self or soul. That is the central purpose and meaning of life. To *that*, everything that you experience can be made to minister. Even the most hard and difficult and desperate things can be enlisted in that process of soul-growing.

These hard and difficult things are, in fact, designed to that very end. The meaning of the universe is a spiritual meaning. It, too, is concerned with souls or personalities, more than with anything else.

This world is not designed to be a bed of roses, or a place where men and women can simply sleep. It offers nothing that is lastingly satisfying to the lounger, the scrounger, or the mere pleasure-seeker. But it *is* designed as a place where men and women can grow souls. And the things by which our souls may grow are the great basic virtues — love, kindness, loyalty, fidelity, courage, truth, fellowship and service.

These things, again, are not just accidents; they are not of value just to *us*. They are among the final realities. The universe too cares about them. The Power behind the universe cares about them. And that Power cares for *us*, and means well by us.

Through all the tangled ways of life, it is an almighty love that is keeping us — a love that cares too much about us to make us soft, but whose design and intention for us is one of absolute goodness and beneficence.

If, to the psychological methods outlined and recommended in this book, you can add such a faith, you have then a combination that is invincible. You have the secret of strong and victorious living. You have hold of truths that matter more than anything else on earth.

Neither money, nor power, nor social position, is anything like so important as the possession of these. With these you have the keys to life — life with all its powers of wonder, beauty, zest and enjoyment. And the future lies before you with its ever-opening doors.

May you have good voyaging as you go onward into this adventure of building a worthwhile self — the most alluring, fascinating and profitable business in which human beings can engage.

POINTS TO REMEMBER

1. — *Psychology has made it clear that some qualities, some kinds of conduct, pay, They pay in terms of happiness, health, wholeness.*

2. — *A religious view of life assures us that these same qualities are not accidental things, but are part of the final truth about the universe. What is psychologically wise links up with what is ultimately true.*

3. — *What we call life is designed to one end — the building of souls or personalities. Every experience can be made to minister to this.*

4. — *The Power behind the universe means well by us, cares about us; and will safeguard those things that we feel to be noblest and most precious.*

Other recommended books...

EFFECTIVE WORDPOWER

Jacqueline Dineen. Do you find difficulty in expressing yourself? Are you puzzled by some of the 'long words' used by others? We are judged by the way we use words, yet it is surprising how limited some people's vocabularies are. In all walks of life, both at work and at leisure, success lies in the ability to use words to advantage, and if you are without a good knowledge of them you will be faced time and again with the exasperation of not being able to say what you mean. In this book the author shows you how to learn more words through reading and listening, and she gives advice on spelling, pronunciation and remembering.

HOW TO RELAX

Wilfrid Northfield. How to acquire the benefits of complete relaxation. Author reveals how to regain lost self-control, become less impatient, enjoy tranquility, meet life with optimism and increase energy for work and play. Serenity, poise and increased efficiency can be ours through relaxation. This book contains a message that none of us can afford to ignore. The demands of modern living, particularly in towns and cities, are such that almost everyone suffers from some sort of tension. It is an occupational hazard. *Contents include:* Rhythmical breathing; Let yourself go; Importance of leisure; Sense of purpose; Anyone can relax; Thought control; The benefit of laughter; Banish anxious thoughts; 'Exciting' colours; Waste of nervous energy; The 'monotonous' job; Message to housewives.

CONQUERING NERVOUS TENSION

Wilfrid Northfield. Millions of people fail to get the best out of life because of 'nerves'. They wake up tired; jump at the slightest sound; cannot concentrate; and lie awake at night, worrying. Nerves are the connecting link between brain and body, like an intricate system of telegraph wires. There are cases of disease in the nerves, but these are comparatively rare. When your nerves are wrong it does not mean that these physical 'telegraphs' are diseased, but that the messages running along them are 'tied up in knots'. The purpose of this book is to 'unravel' these knots. *Contents include:* Secret disease of today; Learn to relax; Excessive nervous tension; Mental control; Energy reserves; Mind-wandering; Nature's energy-rhythm.

CONFIDENT SPEAKING

Margaret Perkins. Speech, to be readily understood anywhere in the British Isles, ought to conform as nearly as possible to what is known as standard English. We must retain our individuality, but when the occasion demands we should be able to speak fluently, without undue accent. By improving our voices and speech we find a more fitting outlet for our personalities. Then attention can be focused on the content and manner of speech, but—as with learning to play a muscial instrument—certain techniques need to be acquired before a melodious tune can be produced. *This book explains:* Consonants; Vowels; Pronunciation and emphasis; Modulation; Phrasing and pause; Correct breathing; Projecting your image; Posture. Includes some hints on public speaking.

THE CONQUEST OF FEAR

W. J. McBride. *In life, as in golf, most people are beaten by 'bogey'!* Yet well over 90 per cent. of the average person's fears are imaginary, arising from the stress and strain of our modern world and the exacting nature of contemporary civilization. Do *you* suffer from irrational fears and phobias; an inferiority complex; incapacitating anxiety; emotional distress; compulsions and obsessions; dread of what the future holds? All these conditions are symptoms of the neurotic fear which afflicts one person in ten of the population! The author traces the origins of these worries, explains their development and provides guidelines for their alleviation and eventual control. The close link between irrational fear and inferiority is also discussed and self-treatment outlined.

CONQUER SHYNESS

C. H. Teear, B.A. Shy people are frightened people because they are always unsure of themselves; they are unable to go out and enjoy a proper social life. They feel themselves to be separated from others by a psychological barrier which is wholly self-erected and which usually has its origin in some unfortunate childhood experience. This book presents a plan of campaign to help those afflicted with shyness to understand themselves and take practical steps for overcoming their handicap. *Contents include:* The urge for friendship; Analyzing your childhood; The centre of attention; Live longer and happier; Trembling and blushing; Magnetic personalities; The opposite sex; Possessive friendship; Building up friendships; Coping with unkindness; Entering and leaving a room; Listen to others.

MAKING FRIENDS EASILY

C. H. Teear, B.A. Loneliness can be experienced in a crowded urban complex! Author reveals psychological 'blocks' which stop us making friends, gives practical measures for developing a positive personality, gaining new interests, banishing selfconsciousness. Nearly all the barriers existing between ourselves and neighbours are of our own making. This book explains how to demolish them once and for all! *Contents include:* Good friends are loyal; The face of friendship; Anti-social behaviour; When the mind turns inwards; Spirit of comradeship; This is a gentleman; Be a good listener; The value of small talk; Don't be a butterfly; Meeting new people; Admit your own faults; The old and the sick; Opportunities through the local church; Keep your sense of proportion.

DYNAMIC MEMORY TECHNIQUES

Jacqueline Dineen. The basic necessities for a good memory are concentration, observation and interest. These powers can be improved beyond recognition by a number of established techniques which are revealed in this book. Memory aids convert abstract thoughts into pictures and these—like photographs taken by a camera—are stored away by the memory for future use. *Contents include:* Mental blanks; Remembering people and what they say; Improving observation; Improving concentration; Reading and studying; Visualization; Learning by listening; Memorizing names; Dealing with difficult names; Remembering facts about people; The peg word system; Using a chain of links; Remembering written material.